Bunnies, Bonnets, and Hot Cross Buns

The History, Legends, and Lore of Easter

By Christopher Forest
Outback Books

Dear readers,

Thanks so much for reading this edition of Outhouse Books. In *Bunnies, Bonnets, and Hot Cross Buns,* you will learn about the history of one of the most popular and important holidays – Easter. From facts about Easter's origins, to trivia about eggs, and little known folklore, this book will turn you into an Easter expert in a matter of hours.

Hopefully you enjoy this brand of specialized reader. It is designed for those of you who like to have a sense of accomplishment, but have limited time to read. These quick readers can be completed in one session....even in the privacy of your own "outhouse."

We hope you enjoy! Happy reading!!! And Happy Easter!!!

Sincerely,
The Outhouse Staff

Outhouse Books
A division of Outback Books

Summary: A collection of interesting facts, trivia, legends, and lore about Easter.

Author: Christopher Forest
Editor: Melissa Forest

ISBN: 978-1497575509

Easter History

"Easter spells out beauty, the rare beauty of new
life."
- S.D. Gordon

Easter is the oldest Christian holiday. Most priests would consider it to be the most important holiday, too. It commemorates Christ's victory over death. While some may ask, "Why did Christ have to die?" Christians will explain that it was the way for people to gain entrance into heaven.

The name Easter probably comes from the pagan holiday, Ostara, which marked the beginning of spring. This holiday was connected with Eastre, a goddess. Bunnies, hares, and eggs were symbols of this goddess.

Do you participate in *pysanka* during Easter? Well, many people do. *Pysanka* is the official name for the act of painting or coloring Easter eggs. The term comes from the Ukraine.

Easter gained strength as a holiday in America following the Civil War with many people looking for rebirth and renewal in the country.

German settlers first brought the idea of the Easter Bunny to America following the Revolutionary War. It is believed the first region of America to celebrate the holiday was Pennsylvania.

Why a bunny? The bunny was originally a pagan symbol for the goddess Ostara, hence its association with spring holidays. As time went on, it became a symbol for ancient Germans celebrating Easter.

Palm Sunday is observed by Christians the week before Easter. It commemorates the arrival of Jesus into Jerusalem to celebrate Passover. So why is it called Palm Sunday? It was tradition for Romans to place palms in the path of people they considered a hero. As Jesus entered the city, palms were placed in front of him.

The practice of holding an Easter parade dates back – in part – to the fact that Christians would often walk around in white robes following the period of being initiated into the church around Easter.

Check em' out! Easter parades gained popularity in the mid 19th century when wealthy New York citizens would leave Easter service. Clothed in new duds, they would show off their Easter best by parading down the streets of the city in their clothes. Soon, regular folk were coming to watch these pseudo-parades, which gave way to real parades. Such parades peaked in popularity about one century later.

Easter parades continue throughout the country. The most popular parade is in Manhattan. Each year, people take part in a parade that goes from 49th street to 57th Street.

Easter Week

Easter week consists of several days that are commemorated by Christians

Palm Sunday – this is the Sunday before Easter. Though technically prior to Easter week, it commemorates Jesus entry into Jerusalem.

Holy Thursday – this day is a reminder of the day that Jesus shared Passover with his disciples. It is also the night that Jesus spoke to his disciples and told them how to remember and honor him (with the ceremony now echoes in a mass or service). On this night, Jesus was arrested.

Good Friday – this day honors the death of Christ. Typically, Christ is said to have been hung on a cross at noontime and died at 3:00 PM. Many Christians remain quiet during this three-hour period.

Holy Saturday – this evening, which includes a long and very ceremonial mass or service, is considered the day when all those who are hopeful are waiting for Jesus return.

Easter Sunday – this day commemorates Jesus victory over death and his resurrection.

Once Upon an Easter

❁

"The story of Easter is the story of God's
wonderful window of divine surprise."
- Carl Knudsen

In the year 1307, King Edward I celebrated a golden Easter. He had eggs boiled before Easter, than covered in golden leaf. He gave about 450 of these eggs as gifts to servants.

On April 2, 1512 – Easter Sunday – Juan Ponce de Leon encountered the future state of Florida during his quest to find the Fountain of Youth. In honor of Easter, called *Pasqua Florida*, Ponce de Leon dubbed the land "Florida." The name has stuck to this day.

In 1722, Dutch Explorer Jacob Roggeveen was sailing through the Pacific. On Easter Day, he landed on the island known as Rapanui. He dubbed the island "Easter Island."

Born on Easter Sunday

Muddy Waters — the father of Chicago Blues music — April 4, 1915 (some say 1913, but April 4 was not Easter Sunday that year)

John Ratzenberger — actor famous for playing Cliff in *Cheers* and voice artist in cartoons — born Easter Sunday (April 6), 1947

Paul Rudd — actor who got his first big start in *Clueless*— was born Easter Sunday (April 6), 1969

Melissa Joan Hart — actress who was known as *Sabrina the Teenage Witch* — born Easter Sunday (April 18), 1975

Emma Watson — actress known for her portrayal of Hermoine in the Harry Potter movies — born Easter Sunday (April 15), 1990

In Eastern Orthodox churches, Easter is known as Pascha. Most of these churches use the old Julian calendar to establish the date...not the more modern Gregorian calendar. The date of Pascha can be the same as the date of the non-orthodox Easter and it can as much as five weeks apart.

How Many Words Can You Make Out Of

CHOCOLATE BUNNIES

_____ _____

_____ _____

_____ _____

_____ _____

_____ _____

_____ _____

_____ _____

_____ _____

_____ _____

Easter Symbols

✝

"Easter tells us that life is to be interpreted not
simply in terms of things but in terms of ideals"
- Charles M. Crowe

Eggs are typically viewed as a symbol of rebirth and were used as a sign of spring prior to Easter celebrations. They are part of the Passover Seder, used to honor the idea of rebirth. Such symbolism has been transferred to Christians, who often view the egg as a symbol of rebirth.

The Easter Bunny was first discovered by German immigrants. They brought the custom of the Easter bunny to America. In fact, the original German Easter bunny was a white hare that left colored Easter eggs on Easter morning.

Print it! The first mention of Easter Bunny dates back to a German book printed in 1572. The book suggests that this bunny lays eggs.

In one legend, Eostre's (a goddess whose namesake was used for Easter) pet bird was changed into a rabbit. This rabbit now possessed the ability to lay eggs to amuse children. The idea of the Easter rabbit – or bunny – likely came from this tradition. In some legends, the rabbit lays eggs on her feast day.

Osterhaas (or Osterhase) is the official name of the first Easter Bunny. Derived in Germany, this Easter bunny began the custom of delivering colored eggs. Children would leave baskets and hats in the shape of nests to collect the eggs. Incidentally, Osterhaas was a hare because hares were associated with fertility.

Where did the idea for Easter baskets come from? Probably bird's nests, which make sense. Birds use a nest for their eggs. The original Easter baskets, which looked like nests, were used to house Easter eggs.

The idea of using a true basket for Easter comes from the old-time Christian custom of bringing a basket with food to mass to be blessed.

Easter lilies, otherwise known as "trumpet lilies," first gained popularity at the turn of the 20th century. The lilies were originally native of Bermuda and quickly gained popularity for their spring blooms.

The Easter lily became associated with Easter because its petals face downward. According to legend, the petals do this to honor Jesus. The petals are also said to resemble the trumpet of the Angel Gabriel.

According to stories, following the death of Jesus, white lilies were found growing the Garden of Gethsemane – the garden in which Jesus was arrested.

Prayerful snack! The pretzel is considered – by some – to be an invention connected to Easter. The first pretzels were probably made by an Italian monk around 610 AD. The shape was said to represent a child's arms folded in prayer.

"Bawk, bawk!" Cadbury Crème Eggs™ are the most popular chocolate eggs in the world.

Check out these "Eastery" towns

Chicken, Alaska

Egg Harbor, Wisconsin

Egg Harbor City, New Jersey

Ham Lake, Minnesota

Rabbit Shuffle, North Carolina

Rabbit Town, Alabama

Rabbit Town, Kentucky

Rabbit Town, Maryland

Jellybeans first became popular at Easter during the 1930s.

Jellybeans were first probably developed by Boston candy maker William Schrafft. During the Civil War, to help drum up business, he urged people to send jellybeans to soldiers fighting.

The custom of sharing Easter cards first developed in Victorian England, when sharing greeting cards became popular. Since that time, he popularity has explored. American Greetings™ suggests that Easter is the fourth most popular card-sending holiday

Butterflies have become associated with Easter as well. Their unique life cycle connects to the idea of rebirth. Some people suggest the caterpillar stage is equal to Jesus's early life on Earth. The cocoon stage represents Jesus's death. The butterfly itself symbolizes Jesus's resurrection.

Nice buns!! Hot cross buns became associated with Easter because they were cooked and given to the poor by monks in Europe. Often, this food was shared with the poor during Lent.

Peter who? Peter Cottontail, from the song that bears his name, was in part derived from Peter Rabbit, the beloved character in the Beatrix Potter books.

Must See Easter Movies

Holiday Inn – (1949) clever prequel to *White Christmas* starring Fred Astaire and Bing Crosby as singers at an inn that only opens on holidays...including Easter.

Easter Parade (1948) – classic Judy Garland and Fred Astaire film with songs by Irving Berlin.

The Robe (1953) – tale of the Richard Burton as a Roman soldier who won Christ's robe and then realizes that the robe is changing his life.

Ben Hur (1959) – classic story of Judah Ben Hur (played by Charlton Heston), a Jewish citizen forced to confront Roman authority – and his best friend - at the time of Christ.

King of Kings (1961) – memorable story of Jesus's life and death complete with an epic Sermon on the Mount scene. Captivating performance by Jeffrey Hunter.

Hop (2011) - animated movie about the Easter Bunny who is next in line to become the legendary figure and totally disinterested in fulfilling that role.

Easter Eggs

○

"For I remember it is Easter morn, and love and
life and peace are all new born."
- Alice Freeman Palmer

Christians were once forbidden to eat eggs during Lent. Having one on Easter was a cause for celebration – hence the major connection between Easter and Easter eggs.

Hard boiled??? These eggs are also associated with Easter because Christians were prohibited from eating eggs during Lent. So, any eggs hatched during Lent were hard-boiled and preserved to be eaten later.

Many ancient cultures participated in the art of giving eggs to celebrate spring. These include:

Egyptians
Gauls
Greeks
Persians
Romans

Egyptians were believed to be the first people who gave Easter eggs on Easter. The eggs were associated with Jesus and His resurrection.

Easter eggs were first dyed multiple colors by the Greeks and Romans. Prior to this, the Egyptians and Babylonians colored them red for the beginning of spring.

Members of Eastern Orthodox faiths often paint their Easter eggs red, too. It is to represent the blood of Christ that was shed and His victory over death. The color has become connected with renewal.

Dyed! Natural dyes were once used to color eggs. Here are a few ways people made the colors:

Juice of cherries to make red
Carrots to make yellow
Red onion skins to make purple
Furze (a shrub with a yellow flower) made yellow

Most people believe that it is wise to purchase eggs a week before coloring them. If you refrigerate the eggs, they will peel easier after dyed. And, if you add a half teaspoon of baking soda to the water – so experts say – it will make the eggs easier to peel.

Eggs were sometimes used as a birth certificate. In the 1800s, when it might be hard to get to the nearest town hall following a birth, a hardboiled (and sometimes colored) egg – with a baby's name – might be sent to the town hall and officially recorded.

Easter eggs might be a pagan tradition, but Christians have adopted it as part of their tradition as well. Eggs – and rolling them – are often thought to symbolize the fact that a stone was rolled away from the cave used to house Christ's body.

In central Europe and Germany, it is popular to pierce holes in the top and bottom of raw eggs. The yolk is removed from one hole (by a person blowing into the other hole). These eggs are often painted or decorated and hung from trees...much like Christmas decorations. In Armenia, such eggs might be decorated with pictures of Jesus, the saints, or Mary.

The most valuable Easter eggs are Faberge eggs, created by Peter Carl Faberge. They were commissioned by Russian Czar Alexander III and were a present for his wife in 1886. These first eggs were not ornate, but in fact very simple.

That's quite a yolk: Easter Jokes

Why do eggs have to be careful telling each other jokes?
They might crack each other up.

What do you call an overly nervous Easter Bunny?
a basket case

What type of stories do baby Easter bunnies enjoy?
Cotton tales

How did the Easter Bunny do on his test?
Egg-sellent

Where do eggs go on vacation?
to Easter Island

What do you call an Easter egg that tells jokes?
A yolkster

What sport does the Easter Bunny play on weekends?
Basket-ball

Why did the Easter Bunny cross the road?
to prove that he was no chicken?

Easter Dinner

"I lied on my Weight Watchers™ list. I put down
that I had 3 eggs...but they were Cadbury™
chocolate eggs."
-Caroline Rhea

The idea of eating ham on Easter dates back thousands of years, when meat was served as a meal to introduce spring. In later years, pork that was not eaten before winter was salted and then taken out at springtime. As a result, Easter became the perfect time to eat ham.

What a mouthful! *Paskelbrygg* is the name given to Easter beer that shows up in the Scandinavian region during springtime. The Easter brew is often made of several different types of local brews.

Some people – particularly those in Eastern Europe – eat lamb at Easter. The idea probably comes from the ancient Jewish custom of eating lamb to commemorate Passover – a holiday often linked to Easter. Christians adopted the custom as well. For many years, lamb was the traditional meal of the Pope on Easter.

A *paska* is the name given to Easter bread that is commonly found in Russia. It contains cottage cheese, sugar and raisins. It is put in a special mold as it cooks so it comes out with a cross on the sides and the letters JC raised from the surface. The JC of course is in honor of Jesus.

In Ireland, a traditional breakfast on Easter Sunday is eggs.

People in Hungary sometimes serve Easter meat loaf. This loaf is made of bread, eggs, ham, chopped pork and assorted spices.

Golden bread is a traditional fare for Easter in Ireland. It is similar to American French toast and is considered a favorite breakfast food for the day.

It's the Easter Beagle Charlie Brown™ trivia

Since 1974, this classic Charlie Brown tale has been watched by millions of fans. See how well you know your Easter Beagle trivia?

1. What problem does Woodstock have at the beginning of the show?

2. Why does Sally have to go to the store at the beginning of the story?

3. Who is helping Peppermint Patty color Easter eggs (for the first time)?

4. What does Linus explain to Peppermint Patty about coloring Easter eggs?

5. Why does Snoopy go to the store with Charlie Brown and his friends?

6. What type of sale does the store have when Charlie Brown and his group of friends arrive there?

7. How does Marcie eat her egg at the end of the program?

8. Why is Lucy mad at Snoopy at the end of the show?

It's the Easter Beagle Charlie Brown™ trivia answers

1. His nest has been soaked by the rain and he needs a new home.
2. She has to purchase new shoes.
3. Marcie...who promptly ruins three batches of eggs.
4. It is a waste of time because the Easter Beagle will deliver them.
5. To buy Woodstock a birdhouse...which is turned into a birdhouse bachelor pad
6. Christmas sale
7. Whole — shell and all (with a little salt, of course)
8. Snoopy took all of the eggs she had hidden and gave them away as the Easter Beagle.

Easter By the Numbers

"The Easter Bunny left something for the kids.
You'd think the Energizer Bunny™ would leave
something for Mom."
- Author unknown

The date of Easter, particularly for western churches, varies. It is the Sunday following the first full moon after March 21. The date can fall between March 22 and April 25

The discrepancy with the dates of Easter traces back to the Council of Nicea in 325 A.D. The council created the date to be on the Sunday after the first full moon in spring. However, many Eastern Orthodox churches did not follow along when the calendars changed from Julian to Gregorian.

The average household spends about $131 on Easter candy each year.

At Easter, Americans eat nearly 16 million jellybeans. They could circle the earth three times.

Quite a peep! The most popular Marshmallow Peeps™ are:
1. Yellow
2. Pink
3. Lavender
4. Blue
5. White

According to the Guinness Book of World Records™, the largest-ever confectionary Easter egg was 25 feet tall. It was concocted with a combination of chocolate and marshmallow. It weighed more Easter egg weighed more than 8,900 pounds and required a steel frame inside to support it. Now that's an egg!

How do you eat your chocolate Easter bunny?

76% of people eat it ears first
5% of people eat it feet first
4% of people eat it tail first

It would appear that the remaining 15 % just dig in.

Test Your Bunny Knowledge

Check off your answer.

	YES	NO
1. Bunnies have four eyelids.		
2. Rabbits can stand on their hind legs.		
3. Rabbits cannot throw up.		
4. A group of rabbits is defined as a mob.		
5. The eastern cottontail is the most common species in the U.S.		
6. Rabbits weigh slightly more than bunnies.		
7. Rabbits eat their own droppings.		

Bunny Knowledge Answers

1. No, but they have three.
2. Yes. They do this to see predators.
3. Yes; file under scary, but true.
4. No, they are actually called a herd (if they are domestic) or Warren (if they are wild).
5. Yes...Peter thanks you for this.
6. No. They are the same.
7. Yes, but only at night. These special, edible nighttime droppings are called cecotropes.

Sweets have it! Easter is the second largest holiday where sweets and candy are purchased, at least in the United States. Only Halloween prompts people to purchase more candy. Americans buy about 2 billion dollars worth of candy, which totals more than 7 billion pounds of Easter confections.

About 95% of the Easter Lilies grown for the American market come from ten farms in the region of the California and Oregon border. Prior to 1941, most of the lilies were imported from Japan.

There are approximately 90 million chocolate Easter bunnies produced every year.

When it comes time to make candy, at the height of production, more than 5 million Marshmallow Peeps™ are made each day.

Six minute treat. The typically marshmallow chick takes about 6 minutes to make. However, in the 1950s – when they were introduced by the Just Born™ company – it took about 27 minutes to make one.

Easter Bunny Riddles

1. What do you call a humorous Easter Bunny?

2. What do you call an Easter Bunny that is an all star basketball player?

3. What type of dance does the Easter Bunny love?

4. When might the Easter Bunny get a ticket?

5. What do you call a carefree Easter Bunny?

6. What do you call an optimistic Easter Bunny?

7. What does the Easter Bunny call his wife?

8. What do you call a person who is obsessed with the Easter Bunny?

Bunny Riddle Answers

1. Funny Bunny
2. Hare Jordan
3. The Lindy hop (or the "Bunning Man")
4. When going through a "hop" sign
5. A hare without a care
6. A sunny bunny
7. His Bunny Honey
8. You say they have a rabbit habit

Easter Customs

"What pleaseth me the sweet time of Easter
That maketh the leaf and flower come out."
- Bertran de Born

Some chick! For years, it was customary to dye baby chicks for Easter. Many states have banned this practice.

Good Friday is actually an official holiday in twelve states in America.

In Eastern Europe, it was long a custom to decorate ornate eggs for Easter. The idea gave way to the development of Faberge eggs in Russia.

In Germany, some people make a large bonfire on or around Easter. It is not only a way to celebrate the season, but to welcome spring. In keeping with the spiritualism of the holiday, old Christmas trees are often used as fuel for these fires.

The Easter what? Kids in Sweden don't wait for the Easter Bunny. They wait for the Easter Wizard. Kids also sometimes dress as a wizard or a witch, because it was believed that witches head to Blue Mountain on the night before Easter.

In a similar vain, Swedish children once thought that witches would climb to the top of church towers on the night before Easter. In part, this is where the custom of dressing as witches came from. Children would go, dressed in costume, to friends' houses carrying an Easter card, looking for coins or candy.

In Finland, it is common for people to eat a sweet called *mämmi* on Easter. *Mämmi* is made of rye malt, rye flower, salt, molasses, powered orange peel, and water.

In Moravia, a part of the Czech Republic, they refer to the week before Easter as the following:
Ugly Wednesday
Green Thursday
Good Friday
White Saturday

On White Saturday, it was a tradition for village boys to go through town making noise with wooden rattles to keep – in their minds – Judas away.

Smell my feet? Children in the Netherlands spend Easter going door to door on Holy Thursday to get Easter eggs...a sort of Easter version of Trick-Or-Treating.

In the Ukraine, church bells are silenced between Good Friday and Easter Sunday. Instead, wooden clappers are struck in place of bells

In Ludge, West Germany, it was a custom to roll "Easter wheels" during Easter. The wheels were made of wood and stood six to eight feet in diameter. Straw is stuffed into the wheels and greens were added to the wheels. The wheels were then taken to a top of the hill, set on fire, and released. The wheels that reached the bottom of the hill were considered to be harbingers of good luck.

In the 1800s, it was common for people to exchange cardboard eggs or hollowed out chicken's eggs.

In Aremenia, the day after Easter has been celebrated as the festival of the dead. People bring food to cemeteries to honor the dead. Often, this food is blessed.

Center stage! Itzapala, Mexico, is the home of a yearly Easter festival where plays are put on to audiences that can draw in more than one million spectators. The custom first began in 1833, following a cholera epidemic. The survivors put on a play to give thanks for surviving.

How strict! In Puritan Massachusetts, it was forbidden to celebrate Easter.

Villagers often opened their windows in old England on Easter. The custom would allow the sun to come in – similar to the Son of God – and chase evil out.

The ancient feast honoring Ishtar (which can be pronounced Easter) took place shortly after the spring equinox. This event helped with the establishment of the date of Easter.

Check those clues. In Norway, Easter has become a time when new crime novels are introduced to readers. This custom, called *Paaskekrim*, has existed for some time. No one knows quite why the popularity exists – though people often go on vacation during Holy Week (and may have more time to read) – but it may be because of the connection between Easter and the death of Christ.

An old custom says that people should wear an article of new clothing on Easter to ensure good luck in the coming year. The custom of wearing new clothes, such as shoes, dresses, and hats, is derived from this. Of course, it probably dates back to a day and age where the new year actually occurred around the first day of spring.

In Latvia, it is custom of play a game where people tap their eggs. Players tap the end of one of their eggs against the like end of another person's egg. They continue to do this until one person is left without an egg that has been cracked.

You get egg roll! The White House Egg Roll began in 1878 with president Rutherford B. Hayes and his wife Lucy. Real eggs were used as part of this roll until 1981, when wooden eggs replaced the natural ones.

Your Must See Easter TV Show Checklist

Here Comes Peter Cottontail (1971) DVD: Rankin Bass classic with a claymation approach to the Easter Bunny, who can time travel.

It's the Easter Beagle Charlie Brown (1974) DVD: Classic Peanuts™ show about Charlie Brown and his friends celebrating Easter.

The First Easter Rabbit (1976) DVD: Rankin Bass animated show narrated by Burl Ives about a toy rabbit that comes to life.

The Easter Bunny is Coming to Town (1977) DVD: Part of the Rankin Bass Easter trilogy, this story follows the format of their *Santa Claus is Coming to Town* with Fred Astaire telling the tale of the Easter Bunny

Yogi™, the Easter Bear (1993) DVD: Yogi, the classic bear, helps rescue a kidnapped Easter Bunny

Alvin and the Chipmunks™ Easter Collection (2012) DVD: Alvin and the gang share Easter adventures.

Easter Lore

"At morn, the cherry blooms will be white,
And the Easter bells will be ringing."
- Edna Dean Proctor

According to old legends, all rabbits are said to lay eggs on Easter Sunday.

The pomegranate has become associated with Easter and the resurrection over time. It dates back to the connection between the old myth of Demeter and her daughter, Persephone, who ate pomegranate seeds. As a result, she had to live six months in the underworld, marking the return of fall and winter. When she returned, spring came back, which turned into summer.

In some parts of Europe, dyed eggs, particularly Easter eggs, are buried into the ground. They are thought to keep houses, fields, and property safe throughout the year.

Don't try it at home (unless you have the proper gear and have consulted with experts). It was once believed that the sun danced on Easter morning in homage to Jesus. Others thought that, if you looked at the sun through a sun protective lens, the image of a lamb — in honor of Jesus — would be silhouetted against the sun.

The idea of wearing new clothes on Easter Sunday is an old custom. In the early days of commemorating the holy day, people often tended to lead simpler lives during Lent. This included limited foods, fasting, and wearing the same clothing regularly. When Easter arrived, the clothing would be discarded on that Sunday.

Some people believe that if you don't wear a new pair of clothes on Easter Sunday, you clothes might get spoiled on Easter. What are the biggest offenders? Birds just might drop on them, or a dog might slobber on them.

In the Ukraine, people used to hide Easter eggs in haystacks or in thatched roofs. It was believed to be a preventative cure to high winds.

In England, it was once believed that hanging a freshly baked hot cross bun in a house would protect it during the course of the year and bring good luck.

Easter music is often called Passion music. It developed in Germany years ago. The songs for Easter have since come in many types — joyous on Easter and more solemn for Good Friday.

Word Search

Try to find these Easter words in the word search.

K	B	M	A	L	B	C	G	G	E
B	A	S	K	E	T	R	C	E	S
O	Y	R	P	A	N	B	U	E	S
N	A	E	H	R	Y	U	O	C	O
N	D	T	J	A	T	N	N	S	R
E	N	S	E	T	R	S	N	E	C
T	U	A	S	S	A	E	U	U	R
E	S	E	S	O	Y	T	D	N	B
R	A	O	T	S	U	S	E	J	E
S	L	A	T	S	E	N	R	A	H

BASKET   LAMB
BONNET   HARE
BUNNY   JESUS
CROSS   NEST
EASTER   OSTARA
EGG   SUNDAY

Word Search Answers

	B	M	A	L			G	G	E
B	A	S	K	E	T				S
O	Y	R		A					S
N	A	E	H	R	Y				O
N	D	T		A		N			R
E	N	S		T	R		N		C
T	U	A		S		E		U	
	S	E		O					B
				S	U	S	E	J	
			T	S	E	N			

In some parts of Europe, it was common to put secret messages on eggs to people. The eggs would then be exchanged on Easter.

One legend says that the anemone – a white flower – grew at the base of the cross the night before Jesus died. As a result, anemones have been connected to Easter. The petals also have red marks on them, symbolic of Christ's blood.

Old Easter Sayings

Plant potatoes on Good Friday

If you go swimming in a stream on Easter morning, it will ease your arthritis.

If you crack open an Easter egg with two yolks, the year will be lucky.

If it rains on Easter morning, it will rain the next seven Sundays.

If you wear new clothes on Easter, you'll have luck all year round.

In older times, lions were connected with Easter. It dates back to an old legend that thought lion cubs were born dead. After three days, their mothers breathed life into them...similar to the idea that Jesus was resurrected after three days.

Legend of the Dogwood

One legend says that the dogwood tree is connected to Easter. The legend tells that the dogwood once grew the size of the oak. The wood of one dogwood was used to construct Jesus's cross. As Jesus hung on the cross, he sensed the sadness in the tree. He told the tree that it would never again grow large enough to be used as a cross. Since that time, the tree is never large enough to be cut and turned into a cross. In fact, some people claim that the four-sided leaves resemble the cross and the marks on each petal are to signify nail marks. Further, the center of the flower is said to bear a resemblance to a crown of thorns.

Sources

Archives for Easter. MTU. URL:
http://blogs.mtu.edu/student-abroad/tag/easter/

Do You Know Your Easter Trivia. Redondo Beach Patch
http://redondobeach.patch.com/groups/around-town/p/quiz-do-you-know-your-easter-trivia

Easter Around the World. Factmonster.com. URL:
http://www.factmonster.com/spot/easter2.html

Easter Articles. Information Please.com. URL
http://www.infoplease.com/spot/easter2.html

"Easter: History, Meaning and Observances of Easter."
Religion Facts URL:
http://www.religionfacts.com/christianity/holidays
/easter.htm

Easter Lily. URL: http://aggie-horticulture.tamu.edu/archives/parsons/publication
s/lily/lily.html

Easter Lore and Superstitions. Snopes.com. URL:
http://www.snopes.com/holidays/easter/easterlore
.asp

"Easter Symbols." Chicago Tribune.com. URL:
http://www.chicagotribune.com/sns-holiday-easter-symbols-pg,0,7203396.photogallery

Easter Symbols and Traditions. Factmoster.com. URL:
http://www.factmonster.com/spot/easterintro1.html

Easter Symbols and Traditions – Holidays. History.com. URL:
http://www.history.com/topics/holidays/easter-symbols

Easter Traditions. Traditions and Customs.com. URL:
http://traditionscustoms.com/religion/easter-traditions

Easter Trivia Interesting and Fun Facts About Easter. Fundoo Times. http://easter.fundootimes.com/easter-trivia.html

"Easter Trivia Quiz." Reader's Digest. URL:
http://www.readersdigest.ca/easter/fun/quizzes/quiz-easter-trivia?question=9

Eleven Fact About Easter. Do Something.com. URL:
http://www.dosomething.org/blog/11-facts-about-easter

Five Famous People born on Easter Sunday. Hub Pages. URL:
http://hubpages.com/hub/FiveFamousPeopleBornonE
aster

Fun Facts on Easter. Fun Facts. Org URL:
http://www.fun-facts.org.uk/holidays/easter.htm

"Fun Facts and Trivia: The Origins of 'Easter,' the Bunny,
and Eggs." Lakeville Patch. URL:
http://lakeville.patch.com/groups/opinion/p/fun-
facts-and-trivia-the-origins-of-easter-the-bunny-
and-eggs

"Happy Easter 2003."
http://www.mstarz.com/articles/10494/20130331/
happy-easter-2013-easter-bunny-egg-hunts-
jellybeans-peeps-other-fun-facts-trivia-about-
springtime-holiday-sunday-march-31-2013.htm

"Ponce de Leon Discovers Florida." History.com. URL:
http://www.history.com/this-day-in-
history/ponce-de-leon-discovers-florida

Liturgical Year: Easter Symbols and Food. Catholic
Culture.com. URL:
https://www.catholicculture.org/culture/liturgical
year/activities/view.cfm?id=1270

"Ten Things You might Not Know About Easter"
dailykos.comURL:
http://www.dailykos.com/story/2013/03/30/119812
8/-10-Things-You-Might-Not-Know-About-Easter-
Including-One-Very-Weird-Factoid

"Top Easter Movies for Kids and Families." About.com. URL:
http://kidstvmovies.about.com/od/easter/tp/easte
rtop.htm

"Twelve Fun Facts About Easter." Parkridefly.com. URL:
http://www.parkrideflyusa.com/blog/2012/04/06/1
2-fun-facts-about-easter/

"Why do we celebrate Easter?" Kids Play and Create. URL:
http://www.kidsplayandcreate.com/why-do-we-
celebrate-easter-fun-easter-facts-for-kids/

Varin, Andra. "Easter Traditions: Little Known Facts of
Easter." The Bryan Times April 1, 1987. URL:
http://news.google.com/newspapers?nid=799&dat=1
9870418&id=H7FPAAAAIBAJ&sjid=U1IDAAAAIBAJ&p
g=4941,1929284

Woolsey, Janette and Sechrist, Elizabeth Hough. *It's Time
for Easter*. Philadelphia: Macrae Smith, 1961.

www.ingramcontent.com/pod-product-compliance
Lightning Source LLC
Chambersburg PA
CBHW060406290526
45791CB00002B/630